The King and his Castle

Neuschwanstein

About one hundred and fifty years ago in the kingdom of Bavaria, in the south of Germany, there was a young prince called Ludwig who lived in a castle with his parents and brother, Otto.

One Christmas, Ludwig's grandfather gave him a big set of building blocks. Ludwig sat down on the floor and started to build a model of a famous arch in Munich—not an easy thing for a young boy to do. He really loved playing with the blocks and his grandfather was very proud of him—after all, a lot of important buildings had gone up throughout the kingdom while he was king and he hoped that, one day, Ludwig would continue the tradition of building beautiful castles and palaces himself.

Ludwig is shown here with his brother. In the background is their parents' home, Hohenschwangau Castle.

By the time Ludwig was eight or nine years old, he had already filled a whole sketchbook with drawings of castles.

Building blocks for a little prince

The 'fairy-tale' King

"The youngest and most handsome king ever," was how the people of Bavaria described Ludwig when he ascended the throne as an eighteen-year-old after his father's death. Everybody was very interested in seeing how the young king would rule the country. But Ludwig was not really interested in politics or military things.

Instead, he took himself off to the mountains where he had spent many summers together with his parents. While there, Ludwig wasted no time in drawing up plans for a romantic, 'medieval' castle near his family home. Ludwig wanted to make his dream come true and show everybody how a king should really live—namely, in a castle like the ones built hundreds of years earlier, with lots of towers and turrets. When he was just a young boy, Ludwig wanted more than anything else to live like a knight from the Middle Ages. But he had been born much too late for that! How he looked up to the heroes of the tales he had read—especially Saint George who had bravely fought the dragon!

For Ludwig, his dream world was much more important than anything else. And that is why he has been known as the 'fairy-tale' king ever since. When Ludwig had the Throne Room in his new castle decorated with scenes from tales of old, he even had a picture of Saint George killing the dragon painted on one wall. The dragon stood for all things bad and horrible—and Ludwig also wanted to win over evil, just like his hero.

The picture on the left shows Ludwig soon after he had been told he was to become king. He is standing in front of the throne, wearing a general's uniform and a regal gown.

The perfect spot for a castle

King Ludwig chose a high, rocky site for his new castle, which we now know as Neuschwanstein ('New Swan Stone'). This dates back to the medieval Knights of Schwangau who used to live on that spot. At first, the king had simply wanted to rebuild the castle that had once stood there. But the more he worked on the plans, the bigger his castle became and, when building work finally began, it had developed into one of the largest and loveliest castles in Germany. Neuschwanstein was, however, never completed, as building work stopped soon after Ludwig's untimely death at just forty-one. Only the principal rooms were ever furnished during his lifetime.

Since the king's death, millions of visitors from all around the world have visited the castle. But how many ever stop to think about how difficult it must have been to build such a huge castle on that spot?

First of all, Neuschwanstein was to be a little castle, . . .

. . . on the second set of plans a number of details were added, . . .

. . . and then, a little later on, Neuschwanstein came to look like it does today.

Building begins !

Ludwig was very impatient and wanted to move into his new castle as quickly as possible. This made his architects and builders rush around in circles. Just imagine how much work had to be done even before building work could begin! How do you build such a huge castle six hundred feet up a rock face? How do you get the heavy stones to the top? A road had to be built first of all, winding its way up the mountainside from the valley below. Then the top of the rock had to be flattened, so it was blasted away together with the ruins of the old castle. The most unusual thing though was a steam-powered crane that the king had built on a platform next to the site. The crane was used to lift all the heavy building material to the top of the mountain. Machines of this type had hardly ever been used on a building site before.

And then water was needed, too—lots and lots of water! A pipeline was laid from the mountains down a narrow gorge and up into the castle. The pressure of the water alone, as it drops from a great height from the mountain into the valley, is enough to pump it up right into the castle itself.

Would knights of old have felt at home here?

Although Neuschwanstein was not built in the Middle Ages, there are many things that can also be found in castles that are hundreds of years old.

Neuschwanstein is built on the top of a hill like many medieval castles. This made them easier to defend if ever attacked. From the outside, such castles seem cold and uninviting with their thick walls and battlements for protection. High towers were used as lookouts for spotting an enemy before they reached the castle walls. The king of the castle, the knights, the ladies and the servants would all live in different wings. Then there used to be rooms for storing weapons and food so that they would not run out of supplies if the castle were under attack over a long period. Medieval castles were really like little, self-contained towns.

1 Royal Residence—the principle part of the castle with the King's Apartments and the Throne Room
2 Ladies' Apartments—not used at Neuschwanstein
3 Knights' House—since there were never any knights living in Neuschwanstein, this is simply a connecting building between the Royal Residence and the Square Tower
4 Lower Courtyard—for carriages and other vehicles to turn
5 Upper Courtyard—with the outline of the planned chapel in the paving
6 Gatehouse—in which King Ludwig once had a suite of rooms so that he could watch over the early stages of the building work
7 Square Tower
8 Large Stair Tower—reserved for the king only
9 Small Stair Tower—for the servants

There's a lot to discover in the castle!

Just look at the view—or is it really a painting?

King Ludwig loved the countryside. One of the things he was most worried about during the building of his castle was that the beauty of the countryside could be spoilt. The builders had to be very careful and follow the king's instructions exactly so as not to do anything wrong. Anybody who has ever seen the castle with the mountains in the background cannot help but think how successful this has been. It almost looks as if it could have been painted as scenery for a play.

When going around the inside of the castle the visitor can see how many windows the king had installed so that he would always have a lovely outlook, even when in the state rooms. The wonderful views look as if they are paintings framed by the windows themselves. The king often used to stand and gaze out into the distance, deep in thought. In two directions he could see for miles over the surrounding countryside and, from another side of the castle, he had a view of the steep mountains.

From the balcony off the Throne Room there is a view of Lake Alp and Hohenschwangau Castle. In the Winter Garden, in a different part of the castle, three-metre-high sheets of glass were made especially for the windows—something that was extremely difficult at that time. The king wanted to be able to look out over the wide expanse of Lake Forggen without his view being interrupted by small panes.

Ludwig loved to watch the clouds cast their magic over the countryside.

A Throne Room as big as a church

Anybody looking at the castle from the outside would never believe how ornate the rooms are inside—especially the Throne Room. It really is a feast for the eyes! It looks rather like a church and is just as high, reaching up over three floors. Wherever you look there is something to discover. Take the mosaic in the floor, for example. How long do you think it would take just to count all the individual pieces: there are in fact two million in all! The mosaic is made up of pictures of animals and plants whereas the domed ceiling is painted with stars, with the sun in the middle. Paintings of saints and tales of their adventures decorate the walls. The columns look as if they are made of blue and red semi-precious stones—they are in fact made of cast iron covered in coloured plaster.

The throne itself was never completed. Ludwig wanted it to be decorated with gold and ivory but it is doubtful if he would ever have had enough money for that. On the back wall of the room there is a painting of Saint George whom Ludwig admired so much. The painting here on the opposite page shows what the Throne Room could have looked like, although it was actually built slightly differently.

The mosaic on the floor was carried out in a traditional way and shows animals and plants from different countries around the world.

The Singers' Hall

In many medieval castles there is a large room which stretches up into the roof. It is often called the Great Hall and was where the knights would have held their meetings and banquets. King Ludwig instructed his architects to build such a big and beautiful hall in his castle, too.

The young king loved the opera and after having seen a performance of *Parsifal*, composed by his friend Richard Wagner, he decided to have the hall decorated with scenes from the Parsifal saga. Although of royal descent, Parsifal had grown up in the country as an ordinary person. One day he met a knight and wanted to become one, too. The paintings around the walls depict important moments in Parsifal's life. In one of them, Parsifal is in the Castle of the Holy Grail and sees the cup, or chalice, in which—legend has it—the blood of Christ was collected at the Crucifixion. Parsifal has to complete a number of difficult tasks and, as a result, he grows into a man of knowledge and eventually becomes king of the castle. Ludwig felt very close to Parsifal and Neuschwanstein was to be his own Castle of the Holy Grail.

The picture at the top is a sketch made before painting directly on the walls and shows how carefully preparations were carried out for the frescoes, such as the one the right.

Where did the king sleep?

What do the rooms where Ludwig lived, ate and slept in look like? They are of course much smaller than the Throne Room or the Singers' Hall but are still very impressive. The bedroom in particular was close to the king's heart and he gave precise instructions as to what it was to look like. No fewer than fourteen woodcarvers worked for more than four years to make his dream come true.

The bed, the washstand, the reading chair and the panelling are all decorated with carvings of the highest quality—or tracery as this type of woodwork is called. The bed is the most eye-catching of all. Not only does is have masses of little spires which make us think of a church, but it is also especially big! King Ludwig was a very tall man, being almost 6'6".

The young king was often sad and lost in his daydreams. Perhaps that is why he had scenes from another opera, *Tristan and Isolde*, painted on the upper part of the walls in his bedroom. The tale is a very sad one: Tristan and Isolde fell in love with each other but, all through their lives, they were never allowed to be together. Only after they had died could they be really happy.

No expense was spared in the king's castle not only for paintings and carvings but also for other luxurious things. He even had a flushing toilet in its own little room off the bedroom and running water in the washbasin. If you pull a knob on the washstand, hot water comes out of the swan's beak and flows into the basin below. The bowl could then simply be tipped and it would empty into an in-built drain.

There is also a small chapel off Ludwig's bedroom. The patron saint of this chapel is St. Louis (the French name for Ludwig) in memory of King Louis of France.

Why is there a cave inside the castle?

From the living room on the third floor of the castle, there are wonderful views over the surrounding countryside. But leading off it there is a small room that has no windows at all. It is certainly a strange feeling suddenly to find oneself in a cave! King Ludwig was known to have sat here at the table with its little barrel of wine all on his own and let his thoughts wander. Then the show would start: he would close the doors behind him so that everything was completely dark and a little waterfall would trickle over the rock face which is, in fact, made of plaster. Hidden coloured bulbs filled the secret cave with a magic light and mist would rise from concealed openings. Today, such theatrical effects would be easy to create but in those days, more than one hundred years ago, new technical inventions were needed to generate electricity and to create steam.

The cave
(or Venus Grotto)
can be lit
in any colour
of the rainbow
by using different
light filters.

Dinner with the king

Ludwig loved the night and preferred to sleep during the day. He used to wake up in the evening and have breakfast. Lunch was served around midnight and dinner eaten in the early hours of the morning. The cooks and servants who had to work for the king did not have an easy time. On the other hand Ludwig's ministers and other kings and queens were happy not to be invited to dinner!

However, the king never dined alone. Ever since his childhood he had had an unusually vivid imagination—in his mind he dreamed of other guests seated around the table. He used to 'invite' knights and rulers from days of old to join him for dinner. Even though these figures were only in his head, they were served the same food as the king. He also talked to them—mostly in French, according to the servants who listened from behind closed doors.

Down the spiral stairs in the kitchen a few floors below, things looked very different from the king's peaceful, fairy-tale world upstairs. However the cooks' job was made much easier by the most up-to-date technology so that the king's food would always be to his satisfaction. An automatic roasting spit was created, for example, especially for use at Neuschwanstein and a hand-operated lift was installed. The food for the king and his 'guests' could then be pulled up to the third floor quickly so that it would not get cold.

Ludwig's mysterious death

When building work started on Neuschwanstein, King Ludwig was already drawing up plans for Linderhof and Herrenchiemsee palaces. But even these projects did not fully satisfy the king. It seems that his architects could not design new palaces and castles fast enough. Ludwig simply wanted to have more than one royal residence.

But then all building work stopped when Ludwig died suddenly, aged just forty-one.

Ludwig had spent huge sums of money on his building projects. On 12th June 1886, he was arrested in Neuschwanstein Castle. It was claimed that he was mentally ill and therefore no longer in a position to rule the country and was taken to Berg Castle on Lake Starnberg, near Munich.

The next day he went out for a walk with his doctor along the shore of the lake but never returned. A search party was sent out and they soon found the bodies of the king and his doctor in the water. But how did it happen? Did Ludwig drown or was he murdered? Even to this day the mystery has never been solved.

During the last few years of his life Ludwig had seldom been seen in Munich, the capital of Bavaria. But this did not stop thousands of people from lining the streets to see the funeral procession. Everyone seemed to feel that he had been someone special who had had a great dream—a dream of a more beautiful world, a fairy-tale world. Even today, so many years later, the life and work of King Ludwig continue to inspire millions of people who flock to Neuschwanstein Castle. The fairy-tale king, who died so young, continues to live in the hearts of so many.

The Illustrations in this Book:

Front cover: Illustration of Neuschwanstein Castle; photograph (inset) of the castle with Lake Alp behind

Title page: Illustration of Neuschwanstein and Hohenschwangau castles with Lake Alp and the Schlicken Mountains

Page 2 top: Friedrich Hohbach, *The Wittelsbach Brothers, Ludwig and Otto: Ludwig with his Sketchbook*, 1854, coloured photograph. Private collection
bottom: Drawing by Crown Prince Ludwig of Hohenschwangau Castle, taken from his sketchbook, 1858. WAF

Page 3: Ludwig builds a model of the Victory Arch in Munich, illustration

Page 4: Ferdinand von Piloty, *Ludwig II in a General's Uniform and Coronation Robe*, 1865, oil on canvas. Ludwig II Museum, Herrenchiemsee. ASV

Page 5: Waldemar Kolmsperger, *Saint George Slaying the Dragon*, 1884, wall painting on the rear wall of the Throne Room. ASV

Pages 6/7 top: The site of the castle with Lake Alp and the Schlicken Mountains
bottom left to right: Christian Jank, *Preliminary design for Neuschwanstein*, 1868; *Upper Courtyard of the castle*, 1871; and *View from the northwest*, 1869; all gouache. Ludwig II Museum, Herrenchiemsee. WAF
main image: Photograph of Neuschwanstein Castle with Lake Alp in the background

Pages 8/9: Neuschwanstein under construction, viewed from the south, November 1881, photograph

Pages 10/11: View of Neuschwanstein, illustration

Pages 12/13
left: The royal toilet
main illustration: Cross-sectional drawing of the castle
top right: In the kitchen

Page 14: Illustration of the castle

Page 15: Photograph from the balcony off the Throne Room over Lake Alp, superimposed with detail from a painting of King Ludwig by Ferdinand Leeke, 1887. Ludwig II Museum, Herrenchiemsee

Page 16: Eduard Ille, *Preliminary design for the Throne Room*, 1876, gouache. Ludwig II Museum, Herrenchiemsee. ASV

Page 17 bottom left and detail top right: Julius Hofmann, *Design for the mosaic floor in the Throne Room*, 1876, gouache. Ludwig II Museum, Herrenchiemsee. ASV
bottom right: Wilhelm Hauschild, *Apsis in the Throne Room*, 1886, wall painting. ASV

Page 18: The vaulted Singers' Hall with a wall painting of the Parsifal saga, photograph. ASV

Page 19 top right: August Spieß, *Parsifal first learns about Chivalry*, 1883/84 (detail), sketch for a wall painting